LAND TRAVEL

Curriculum Consultants

Dr. Arnold L. Willems
Associate Professor of Curriculum and Instruction
The University of Wyoming

Dr. Gerald W. Thompson
Associate Professor
Social Studies Education
Old Dominion University

Dr. Dale Rice
Associate Professor
Department of Elementary and Early Childhood Education
University of South Alabama

Dr. Fred Finley
Assistant Professor of Science Education
University of Wisconsin

Subject Area Consultants

Astronomy
Robert Burnham
Associate Editor
Astronomy Magazine and *Odyssey* Magazine

Geology
Dr. Norman P. Lasca
Professor of Geology
University of Wisconsin — Milwaukee

Oceanography
William MacLeish
Editor
Oceanus Magazine

Paleontology
Linda West
Dinosaur National Monument
Jensen, Utah

Physiology
Kirk Hogan, M.D.
Madison, Wisconsin

Sociology/Anthropology
Dr. Arnold Willems
Associate Professor of Curriculum and Instruction
College of Education
University of Wyoming

Technology
Dr. Robert T. Balmer
Professor of Mechanical Engineering
University of Wisconsin — Milwaukee

Transportation

James A. Knowles
Division of Transportation
Smithsonian Institution

Irving Birnbaum
Air and Space Museum
Smithsonian Institution

Donald Berkebile
Division of Transportation
Smithsonian Institution

Zoology
Dr. Carroll R. Norden
Professor of Zoology
University of Wisconsin —
  Milwaukee

First published in Great Britain by Macmillan Children's
  Books, a division of Macmillan Publishers Ltd, under the
  title *Look It Up.*
First edition copyright © 1979, 1981 Macmillan Publishers Ltd
  (for volumes 1-10)
First edition copyright © 1980, 1981 Macmillan Publishers Ltd
  (for volumes 11-16)
Second edition copyright © 1985, 1986 Macmillan Publishers Ltd

Published in the United States of America

Text this edition copyright © 1986 Raintree Publishers Inc.

Library of Congress Number: 86-641

 2 3 4 5 6 7 8 9 0   90 89 88

Printed and bound in the United States of America.

Library of Congress Cataloging-in-Publication Data

Let's discover land travel.

  (Let's discover; 12)
  Bibliography: p. 69
  Includes index.
  Summary: A reference book dealing with the various ways
man travels on land, from carts and bicycles to trucks and
subways. Includes a section on roads, bridges, and tunnels.
  1. Transportation—Juvenile literature. [1. Transportation]
I. Title: Land travel. II. Series.
AG6.L43 vol 12, 1986   [TA1149]   031s [629.04'9]   86-641
ISBN 0-8172-2611-7 (lib. bdg.)
ISBN 0-8172-2592-7 (softcover)

LET'S DISCOVER
LAND TRAVEL

RAINTREE PUBLISHERS
Milwaukee

Contents

THE HISTORY OF LAND TRAVEL

These pictures show how land travel has changed. At first people carried heavy loads. Then they rolled them over logs. Later, wheels were invented. Over the years, travel became easier and easier. Now we have cars, trucks, and trains.

carrying loads on poles

pack animals

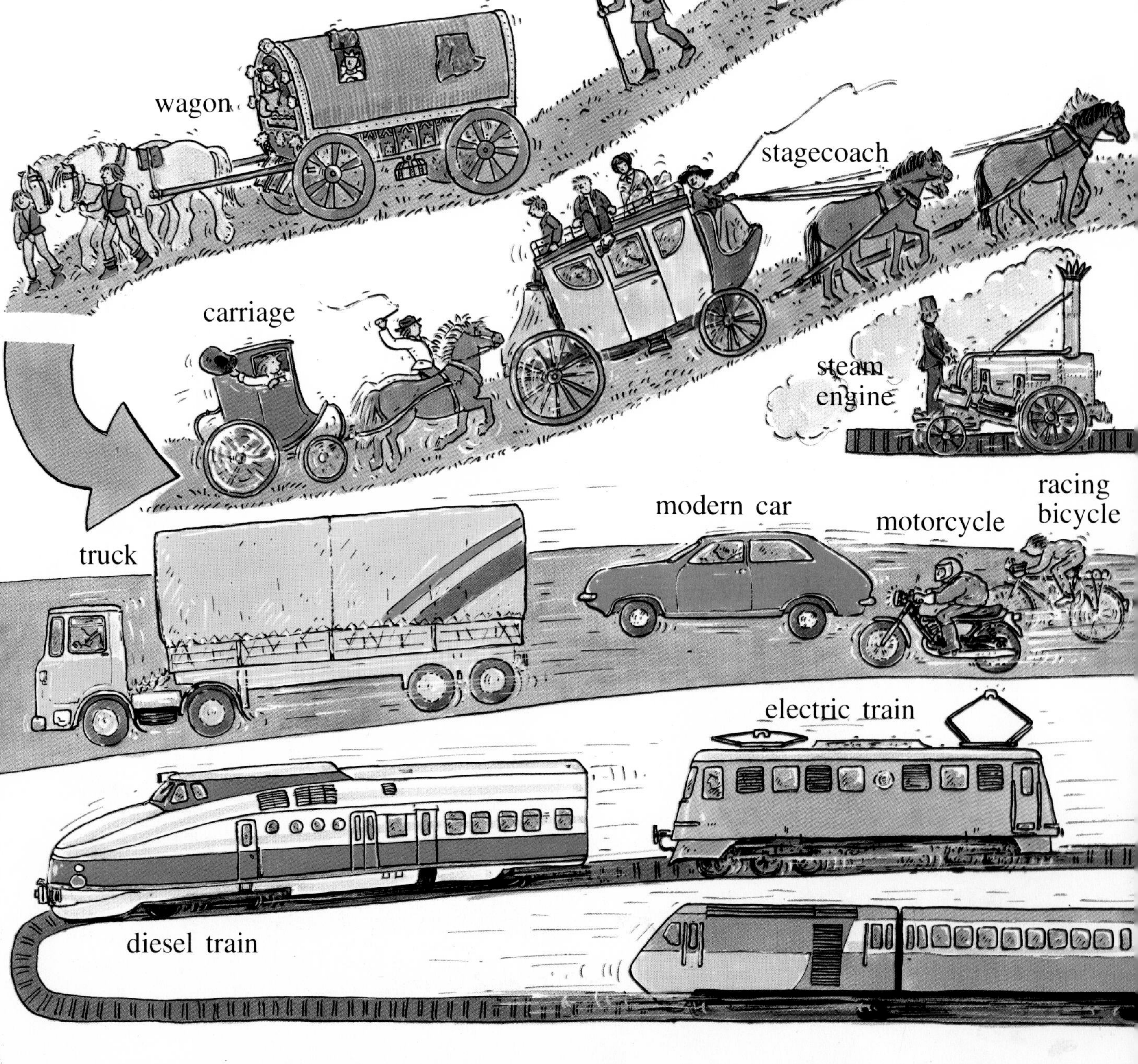

wagon

stagecoach

carriage

steam engine

modern car

motorcycle

racing bicycle

truck

electric train

diesel train

rolling stones over logs

wheeled wagon pulled by animals

early bus

early bicycle

early car

early steam train

early bus

safety bicycle

Model T Ford

steam train

high-speed train

7

Early travel

People rode on animals long before wheels were invented. They used animals to carry goods too. Animals had to be tamed before they could be used to carry loads.

In some countries animals are still used to carry people and goods.

Llamas are used in hilly parts of South America. They can walk safely on rough and steep mountain paths.

Camels can travel in the desert. Their wide feet keep them from sinking into the soft sand.

Reindeer pull sleds over soft snow in Lapland. Several reindeer may be used to pull a heavy load.

Horses, donkeys, and mules can carry heavy loads over bad roads. They wear iron shoes.

Elephants can carry people and goods. They can carry very heavy loads.

Carts, wagons, and stagecoaches

No one knows who invented the wheel. It made travel much easier. The first wheels were solid wood. They were heavy. Later, people learned to make light, strong wheels.

At the right is a Roman wagon pulled by horses. The wheels had spokes.

This Indian cart is pulled by bulls. Wheels like these were invented about 7,000 years ago.

Long ago there were no trains and roads were poor. People traveled from town to town by stagecoach. It took all day to travel 50 or 60 miles.

Stagecoaches like this one crossed the American continent about 100 years ago. It was a bumpy and dusty ride. Some stagecoaches carried mail too.

Posters like this one told people about stagecoaches.

CALIFORNIA STAGE CO.

OFFICE, ORLEANS HOTEL,
SECOND STREET, BETWEEN J AND K,
SACRAMENTO.

J. BIRCH, - - - PRESIDENT.

DAILY CONCORD COACHES

Leave the Orleans Hotel, Sacramento, carrying the U. S. Mail, viz:

Marysville and Shasta,

Touching at

Charley's Rancho, Bidwell's Rancho, Hamilton City, Oak Grove, Clear Creek, Lawson's, Tehama, Campbell's Rancho, Red Bluffs, Cotton Wood Creek, One Horse Town, Middletown, Covertsburg, Shasta, Yreka and Pitt River Diggings.

TWO WHEELERS

Early bicycles

The first bicycles did not have pedals. Riders sat on a wooden beam. They pushed themselves along with their feet. These early bicycles had wooden wheels. Later, metal was used and pedals were added.

The Hobby Horse was a bicycle without pedals. It was used in Europe about 150 years ago.

This bicycle was used about 100 years ago. It was difficult to ride.

Cycling was very popular before cars were invented. People used bicycles of all kinds for travel and for fun.

Motorcycles

The first motorcycles were made over 100 years ago. In France, Pierre Micheaux put a steam engine on his bicycle. A few years later, a German named Gottlieb Daimler used a gasoline engine to power his bicycle. Motorcycles soon became popular.

Daimler's motorcycle is shown above. This machine showed how engines could be used.

Motorcycles with sidecars were once used for family travel. Now most of them are used for racing, like the one below.

Today, the Japanese are the most famous motorcycle makers. They make motorcycles of all sizes. Some are small enough for very young children, like the six year old girl at the right. Riders wear a helmet for safety.

Metro (Great Britain)

Mustang (U.S.A)

Citroen (France)

CARS

Cars are made in many parts of the world. Many countries make cars that are sold in other countries. These are just a few of the cars you can see today. See the line coming from each picture? It points to the place on the map where the car is made.

Alfa Romeo (Italy)

Saab (Sweden)

Toyota (Japan)

Audi (Germany)

Cars come in different sizes for different purposes. The Mini is a good town car. It is small and easy to park. The Volkswagen is a station wagon. It is good for big families. It can carry a lot of people. Some people like a very fast car, like the Alfa Romeo.

Early cars

Many of the first cars looked more like wagons or carriages. Others looked like bicycles. But they all had engines. The wheels were often made of wood, with solid rubber tires. Many of them had no tops to keep the rain off. They must have been very cold in the winter.

early car

Stanley Steamer

The earliest successful cars were made about 100 years ago. German engineers designed and built them. Karl Benz made the three-wheeled car below.

The Stanley Steamer was faster than many gas cars. It was driven by steam power.

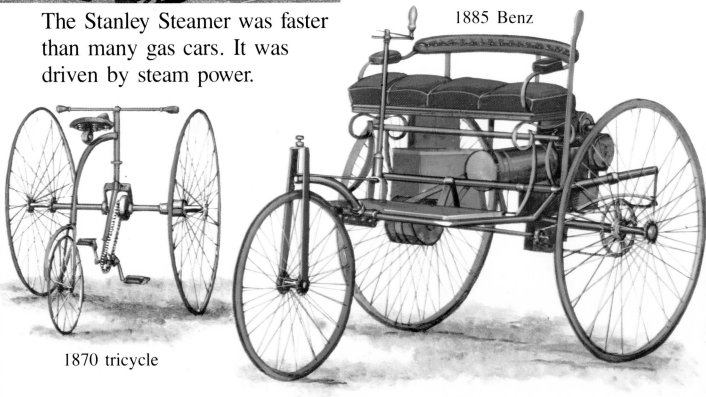

1885 Benz

1870 tricycle

1903 Daimler

This car was made by Gottlieb Daimler. It was driven by a gas engine.

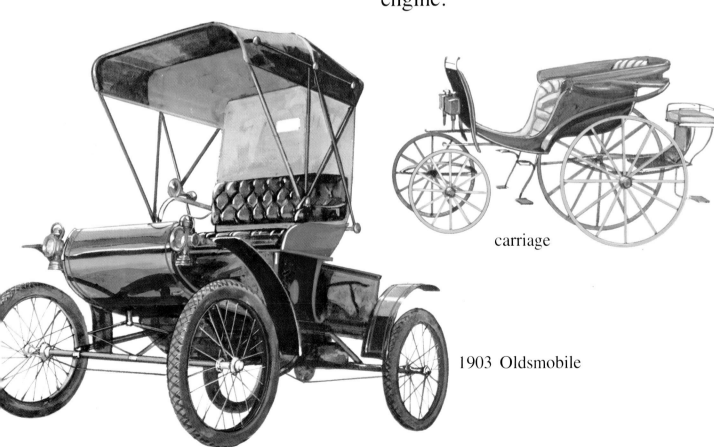

carriage

1903 Oldsmobile

Early motoring

The first cars were built for rich people. They cost a lot of money. Speed limits were sometimes only 5 miles per hour. At first the noisy cars frightened people and animals. They seemed so big and powerful.

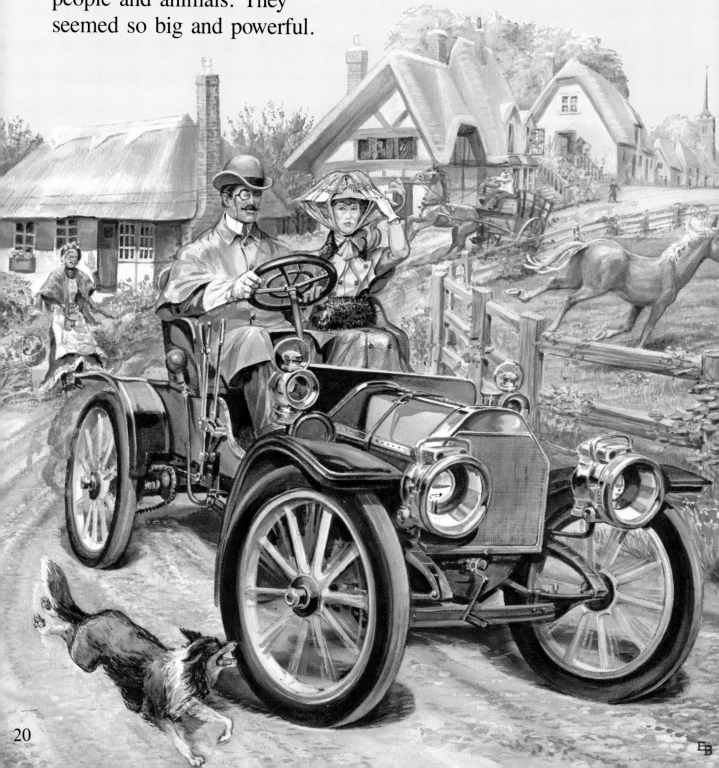

1919 Model T Ford

Henry Ford decided to make a cheaper car. He wanted a car that working people could afford to buy. He built the Model T Ford. In 19 years he sold about 15 million of them. Other companies also made cheaper cars. At the right is an early Austin, made in England.

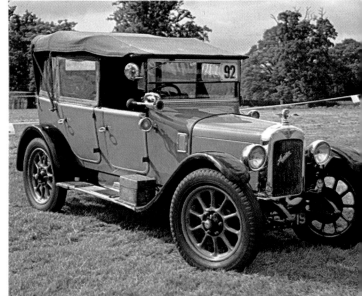

Special vehicles

Have you ever tried riding a bicycle over a muddy field? It is difficult. Cars and trucks get stuck in mud and snow. Special vehicles are made to travel over difficult ground. Some are used for special jobs. The machine at the right helps harvest fruit.

Earth movers help to build roads. They have big wheels and can dig and push the earth.

The beach buggy can be used on sand. It has a small powerful engine and very wide tires. It is fun to drive.

The snowmobile is used for traveling over snow. People who work in the Arctic use it to get around. People use snowmobiles for fun too.

Racing cars

In the U.S. the first motor car race was the Times-Herald race in Chicago in 1895. The most famous type of car racing today is called Grand Prix. This picture shows a Grand Prix race about 50 years ago.

R Phillips 79

Go-carts are very small racing cars. They can travel about 40 miles per hour. Go-carting is great fun.

Stock car racing uses the same kind of cars you can see on roads. Sometimes drivers in a stock car race have to go over very rough ground.

Land speed records

A Frenchman named Rigolly held the land speed record at the end of the last century. He drove an electric car at 97 kilometers (60 miles) per hour.

Thrust 2

The land speed record is held by Richard Nobel, an Englishman. His car is called Thrust 2. He drove it 1,020 kilometers (634 miles) per hour.

Thrust 2 was powered by an airplane engine. In 1970, Gary Gabelich drove his Blue Flame at 1,001 kilometers (622 miles) per hour. The Blue Flame was powered by rockets.

VANS AND TRUCKS

There are many different kinds of vans and trucks. All of them are made to do certain kinds of jobs. What jobs do these vehicles do?

tank truck

mini bus

delivery van

street sweeper

refrigerator trailer truck

fire engine

flatbed truck

car transporter

Caterpillar transporter

dump truck

ambulance

garbage truck

bus

builder's truck

land rover

CA

29

Trailer trucks

Trailer trucks have two parts. The engine and the driver's cab form one unit. This is joined to a trailer. Heavy loads are carried on the trailer. The vehicle below has a flatbed trailer. It has no sides or top. The trailer at the right is covered.

This trailer is a tank with
wheels. Tank trucks carry
liquids, such as oil or milk.

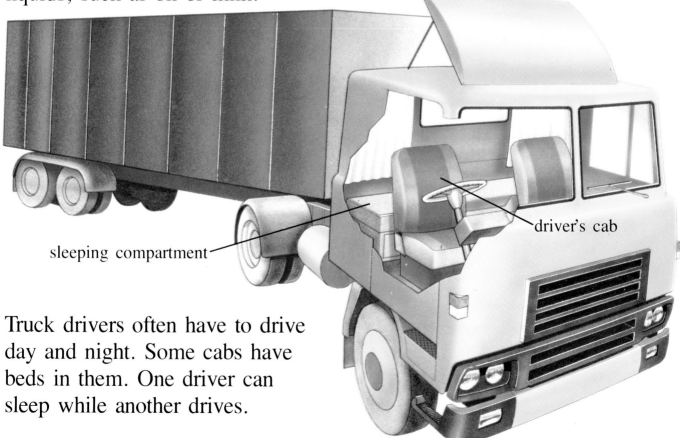

sleeping compartment

driver's cab

Truck drivers often have to drive
day and night. Some cabs have
beds in them. One driver can
sleep while another drives.

Heavy loads

Sometimes very heavy loads have to be moved by road. Special transporters and flatbed trailers are used. A special flatbed trailer with many tires was used to carry the Space Shuttle. The Space Shuttle was one of the biggest things ever moved by road.

An earth-moving machine moves very slowly. It can be moved much faster on top of a big flatbed trailer.

This is a car transporter. The cars are carried on two levels. How many cars can it carry at one time?

Space Shuttle

BUSES

Nearly every country in the world has buses. They are made in many shapes and sizes. Some are double deckers, like the London bus below. The bus at the right has an open top. Passengers get a good view of the countryside as they travel along.

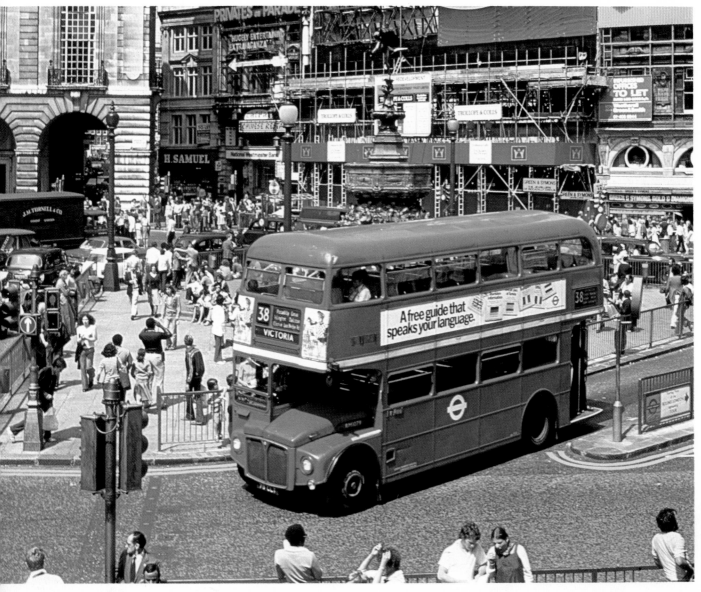

These people are boarding a bus in Sierra Leone in western Africa. Their belongings are carried on the roof.

Early buses

Big buses today can carry as many as 80 people. The first buses were much smaller. Some were pulled by horses. Others were driven by steam engines.

The first city bus systems started over 150 years ago.

This was the first bus service in France. People could ride inside or on top of the bus. It was pulled by four horses.

steam coach

The first steam coach service was started at about the same time as the first buses. A steam engine pulled a coach.

The first double deckers had no roof over the top deck. Riders at the top would get wet when it rained.

1923 London bus

Motor coaches

Motor coaches are faster and more comfortable than city buses. It is cheaper to travel by motor coach than by train or airplane.

Big motor coaches travel day and night. People can sleep in their seats at night. The buses stop for meals.

Many people spend vacations on coach tours. They travel from place to place by coach and stay in different hotels. People can enjoy the scenery through the big windows.

Seventy years ago, families enjoyed trips in coaches like this. You can see these coaches in museums.

ROADS

Early roads

The Romans built thousands of miles of roads. They used big, flat paving stones.

This street is made of rounded stones called cobbles. Many old towns and cities have cobblestone streets. They are very slippery in wet or icy weather.

Most roads were just muddy tracks 500 years ago. Carts and wagons often got stuck.

About 200 years ago better roads were built. People paid a toll at the turnpike gate to use the road.

turnpike

Highways

Highways like this are called superhighways or expressways. Cars travel at high speeds. Walking or parking along the highway are not allowed. Special ramps allow vehicles to get on or off the highway.

Bridges

Bridges cross waterways and deep ditches. Many roads go across bridges. There are three main kinds of bridges. They are the beam, the arch, and the suspension bridge.

This long beam bridge crosses a lake. A number of beam bridges have been joined together.

This is an arch bridge. The curved arch holds up the roadway. Arches are made of stone, concrete, or steel.

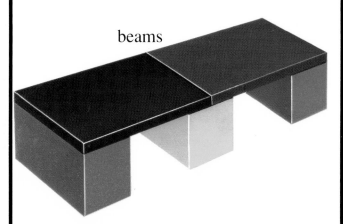

beams

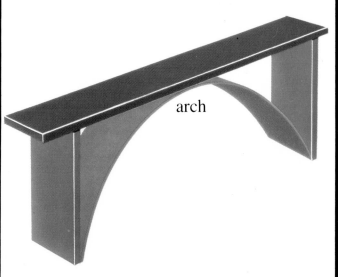

arch

You can make a beam bridge with bricks and beams of wood. Keep the beams short. A long beam will sag in the middle.

Make an arch bridge with cardboard. Make another with no arch. What happens if you put a heavy stone on the bridge without the arch?

This is a viaduct. It has a number of tall arches joined together. This train crosses a steep valley on the viaduct.

This is a suspension bridge. The road is suspended, or hung, from steel cables. Tall towers hold the cables.

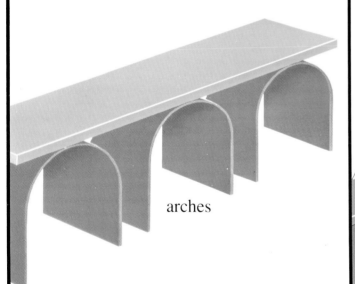

arches

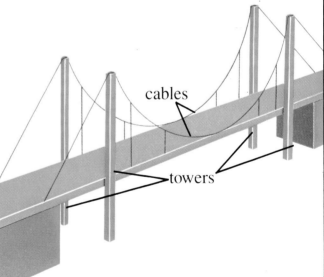

cables

towers

Make a model viaduct. Use stiff paper. Is this bridge as strong as your models of the single arch or beam bridges?

The weight of the suspension bridge rests on the towers. The steel cables are fixed into the ground at each end.

Tunnels

Tunnels take roads under the ground or through hills. They are also built for railways. The Mont Blanc tunnel is over 7 miles long. It goes from France to Italy through the mountains. It was cut through solid rock.

This engineer is blasting through rock to build a tunnel. Holes are drilled into the rock. Explosives are packed into the holes and blown up.

When a tunnel is built through clay or soft earth, a metal frame is used. This is called a shield. A tunnel lining is built behind the shield to hold up the roof.

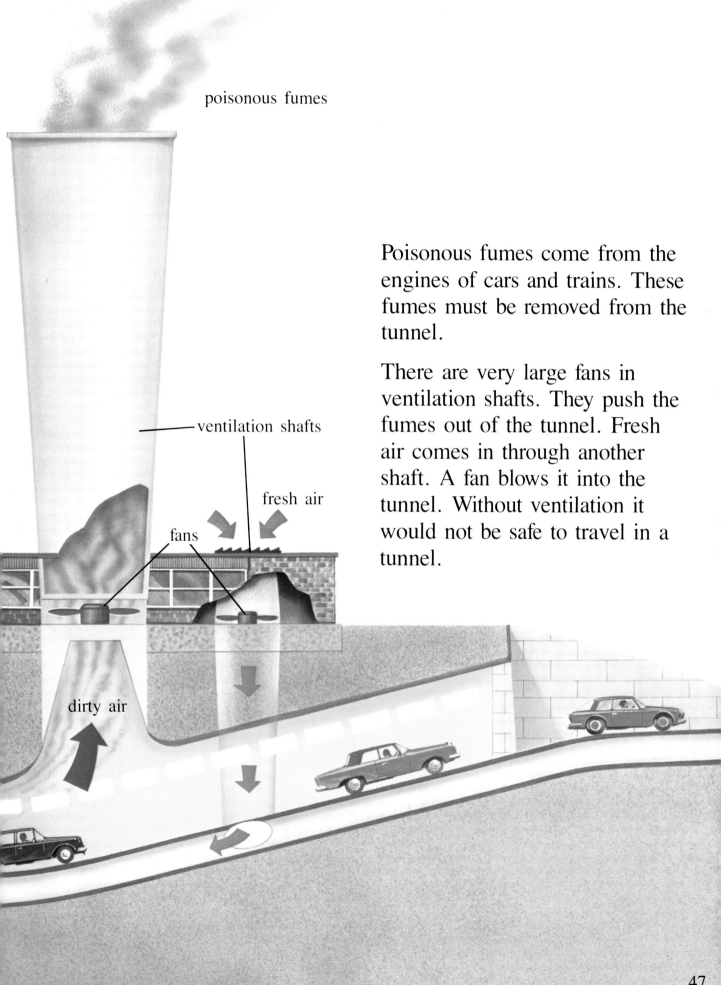

poisonous fumes

ventilation shafts

fresh air

fans

dirty air

Poisonous fumes come from the engines of cars and trains. These fumes must be removed from the tunnel.

There are very large fans in ventilation shafts. They push the fumes out of the tunnel. Fresh air comes in through another shaft. A fan blows it into the tunnel. Without ventilation it would not be safe to travel in a tunnel.

RAILWAYS

Passenger trains

Millions of people travel by train every day. Trains are safer and more comfortable than most cars. Train stations are busy places.

On many trains you can eat in a dining car.

an early dining car

The world is becoming short of oil and gas. In time, more people may travel by train instead of driving cars. A train can carry hundreds of passengers. Trains use less fuel per passenger than cars. The train below carries people on two levels.

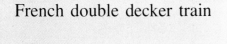

French double decker train

Freight trains

The first railways were built to carry coal and other heavy goods. Trains that carry goods are called freight trains. Special transporters like those at the right are used to carry new cars from car factories.

Sometimes one engine is used to pull a train of 40 or more freight cars. This is a freight train traveling through Canada.

This is a container depot in Germany. Freight trains are loaded and unloaded here. A big crane is used to pick up the heavy containers.

Locomotives

The engine car of a train is called a locomotive. The first locomotives were steam powered. Steam engines are still used in a few countries. Most countries now use diesel and electric locomotives. These are stronger and faster.

Electric trains do not have to carry their fuel. Power comes from electric cables overhead.

This is a steam locomotive in India. Burning coal or wood makes water boil in the engine. This makes steam, which drives the wheels.

This modern locomotive is powered by two diesel engines. Diesel engines burn oil.

Special railways

The first railways were built to help workers in mines. Some railways are still used for special purposes. The railway at the right is used in a coal mine. Cable cars are used on steep mountains. It is difficult to build a railway up a steep mountain.

cable car

This little train has special tracks
and wheels that help it climb up
steep hills.

Early railways

Puffing Billy, at the right, was built in 1813. It is one of the oldest steam locomotives in the world. Puffing Billy pulled coal wagons at a coal mine in Newcastle, England. It was used for 50 years. Now it is in a museum in London.

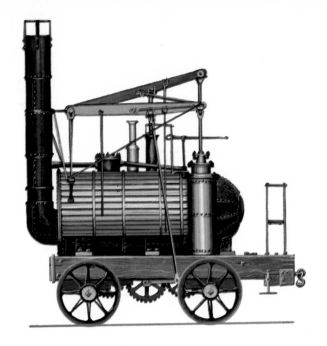

The first steam train to run in Germany was called the Eagle. It is on the left.

The engine below was called Tom Thumb. It was built in the United States. This engine had a race with a horse. The horse won.

The first railway for passengers
was opened in 1830. It ran
between two cities in England.
Its engine, called the Rocket,
was built by Robert Stephenson.

CITY TRANSPORT

Subways

Subways are a quick and easy way of traveling. Many cities have underground trains. This station is in Moscow.

London was the first city to have a subway. The first tunnel was built over 100 years ago. The picture on the right shows how the tunnels link up. Below are some workers building a new subway tunnel.

entrance

northbound tunnel

ticket area

gate

passageway

escalator

eastbound tunnel

westbound tunnel

southbound tunnel

Streetcars

Streetcars run along tracks on the street. Sixty years ago there were streetcars in many cities. Some were pulled by horses. Others were powered by steam or electricity. There are still streetcars in some cities today. Cable cars are used to travel over the steep hills of San Francisco. The cars are pulled along by a moving cable under the street.

cable car

POWELL AND MARKET
AQUATIC PARK
MARINE MUSEUM
HYDE BEACH
FISHERMAN'S WHARF
3 BLOCKS
FROM TERMINUS

24

"Meet me at the St. Francis"

The streetcar at the left is used in India. Its steam engine can burn coal or wood.

The trolley below is in Melbourne, Australia. Wires from the car connect with electric cables overhead.

Today there are only a few streetcars left. Most have been replaced by buses. Some cities have trolleybuses. A trolleybus rides on wheels like a regular bus. But it is powered by electricity from overhead cables.

Taxicabs

A quick way to travel in a busy city is by taxicab. Taxi drivers know how to get around in a city. You pay the driver for the ride. Most taxis have a meter that tells you the price of the trip. The farther you travel, the more it costs.

This is a Chinese rickshaw. The driver pushes or pulls the passenger. Some rickshaws are pulled by a bicycle. A rickshaw is slower than a car, but it is fun to ride.

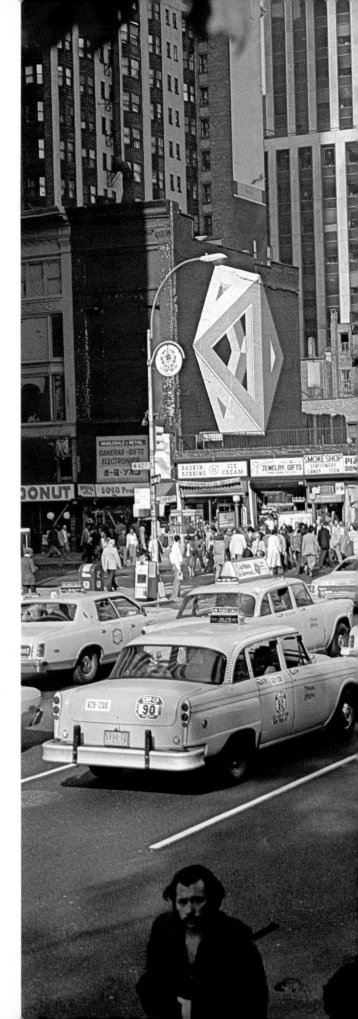

Most taxicabs are painted a special color. This makes it easy for you to spot one on a busy street. The New York cabs, at the left, are yellow. Cabs in London, shown above, are black.

GLOSSARY

These words are defined the way they are used in the book.

Alfa Romeo (AL fuh roh MAY oh) a small, fast car made in Italy

arch (ahrch) a curved structure that is built to support the weight of the material above it

arch bridge (AHRCH brij) a bridge with a curved support holding up the roadway

Arfons, Art (AHR fahns, ahrt) the person who drove the jet-powered racing car, the Green Monster at record speed in 1963

Austin (AWS tihn) a car company that makes small, inexpensive cars

beach buggy (beech BUHG ee) a motor vehicle with large tires, which help it move on a sand beach

beam bridge (BEEM brij) a bridge with columns to hold up the roadway

Benz, Karl (behnz, karl) a German who designed and built cars about 100 years ago

bicycle (BY sih kuhl) a vehicle with two wheels, one behind the other; it has a seat, handlebars to steer with, and two foot pedals to turn the wheels

Blue Flame (bloo flaym) the jet-powered car that set a land speed record in 1970

bridge (brij) anything built across a river, road, or railroad track so that people can get from one side to the other

cab (kab) the front, covered part of a truck or other machine where the driver sits

cable (KAY buhl) a strong, thick rope, often made out of wire

cable car (KAY buhl kar) a car drawn by an overhead cable; it is used to carry people or things up and down a steep hill

camel (KAM uhl) a large animal that has a humped back, long legs, and a long neck; it is found in hot, dry areas

Citroen (SIH truhn) a car made in France

coal (kohl) a black or brown ore used as a fuel

cobblestone street (KAHB uhl STOHN street) a road surface covered with small, rounded stones

container (kuhn TAY nuhr) a box, can, or jar that holds something

crane (krayn) a large machine that can move heavy objects from one place to another

cycle (SY kuhl) to ride a bicycle, tricycle, or motorcycle

Daimler, Gottlieb (DAYM luhr, GAHT leeb) the person who made a small gas engine and used it on a motorcycle

depot (DEE poh) a place for storing goods; also a building for railroad or bus passengers

diesel engine (DEE zuhl EHN jihn) an engine that burns fuel oil instead of gasoline

dining car (DYN ihng kar) the part of a train where meals are served and eaten

double decker (DUHB uhl DEHK uhr) a bus with an upper and lower sitting area

earth mover (URTH moo vuhr) a large machine that can move piles of earth quickly

electric car (ih LEHK trihk kar) a car that is run by electricity

electric locomotive (ih LEHK trihk LOH kuh MOHT ihv) a train engine that is run by electricity

engine (EHN jihn) a machine that uses energy to run other machines

engineer (EHN juh NEER) a person who plans and builds machines and buildings

explosive (ehks PLOH sihv) likely to explode or cause an explosion; a bomb is an explosive device

expressway (ehks PREHS way) a wide highway built for fast and direct traveling

flatbed trailer (FLAT BEHD TRAY luhr) a platform or shallow box pulled behind a truck

Ford, Henry (fawrd, HEHN ree) the person who developed the Model T Ford car

freight train (FRAYT trayn) a train that carries goods or cargo

fume (fyoom) a smoke or gas that is harmful or has a bad smell

Gabelich, Gary (GAY beh lihch, GAR ee) the person who drove the jet-powered car the Blue Flame to a new land speed record in 1970

gasoline (GAS uh leen) a fuel that is made from oil

go-cart (GOH kahrt) a small racing car

Grand Prix (grand pree) a famous car race that is run in Europe

Green Monster (green MAHN stuhr) a jet-powered car that broke a land speed record in 1963

helmet (HEHL muht) a covering for the head that is worn for protection

Hobby Horse (HAHB ee hawrs) a bicycle without pedals that was popular in Britain and France 150 years ago

Lapland (LAP land) an area in northern Europe known for its herds of reindeer and the people who live there

llama (LAHM uh) a large animal that lives in South America; it has a thick, woolly coat

locomotive (LOH kuh MOH tihv) a train engine that moves on its own power; it is used to pull the rest of the railroad cars

Micheaux, Pierre (mih CHOH, pee EHR) the person who invented the first motorcycle

mine (myn) a large open space dug under or into the ground, coal and other materials are dug out of mines

Mini (MIH nee) a small car made in Great Britain and good for city driving

Model T Ford (MAHD uhl TEE fawrd) the first car built in large numbers that people could afford

motor coach (MOH turh kohch) a large, closed carriage that was driven by an engine

motorcycle (MOHT uhr SY kuhl) a two-wheeled machine that is powered by an engine

Mustang (MUHS tang) a car made in the United States

oil (oiuhl) a liquid fuel used to run engines

passenger (PAS uhn juhr) a person who rides in a vehicle

poisonous (POY zuhn uhs) containing poison

railway (RAYL way) large groups of railroad tracks and the trains that run on them

rickshaw (RIHK shaw) a taxi that is either pushed or pulled by a driver; some rickshaws are pulled by a bicycle

Saab (sahb) a car made in Sweden

shield (sheeld) a metal frame built inside a tunnel; it supports the walls and ceiling

sidecar (SYD kar) a seat on the side of a motorcycle for a passenger

Sierra Leone (SEE ehr uh LEE ohn) a country in western Africa

snowmobile (SNOH moh beel) a motor vehicle that has skis and is used to travel on snow

South America (SAUTH uh MAHR ih kuh) the large

continent south of the United States

Space Shuttle (spays SHUHT uhl) a spacecraft that takes off like a rocket but lands like an airplane

spokes (spohks) the parts of a wheel between the rim and the hub

stagecoach (STAYJ kohch) a vehicle pulled by horses; used to carry passengers long ago

Stanley Steamer (STAN lee STEEM uhr) a car that went very fast and was driven by steam

steam (steem) the vapor that water changes into when it is boiled

steam coach (steem kohch) a coach that was pulled by a steam engine

steam engine (steem EHN jihn) an engine that is powered by steam

Stephenson, Robert (STEE vehn suhn, RAHB uhrt) the person who built the train engine called The Rocket

streetcar (STREET kar) a vehicle that runs on tracks on a city street

subway (SUHB way) an underground tunnel in which public trains run

superhighway (SOO puhr HY way) a large, modern road for cars

suspension bridge (suh SPEN shuhn brij) a bridge on which the roadway is hung from steel cables

tank truck (TANGK truhk) a truck that has a large tank; used to carry liquids

taxi (TAK see) a car that carries passengers; another name for a taxicab

taxicab (TAK see kab) a car that carries passengers; another name for a taxi

toll (tohl) the money people pay in order to use a road

vehicle (VEE ihk uhl) something that is used to carry goods or people

Toyota (toy OH tuh) a car made in Japan

trailer truck (TRAY luhr truhk) a truck pulling a trailer; it is used to carry heavy loads

transporter (trans POHRT uhr) a large truck used to carry heavy or special loads; the new cars arrived by transporter

trolley (TRAHL ee) a streetcar run by electric cables overhead

tunnel (TUHN 'l) a hollowed-out space through a hill so that a road or railway can be built

turnpike gate (TUHRN pyk gayt)
the beginning or end of a
turnpike; the place where a toll
is paid

van (van) a large, covered truck
used to move things

ventilation shaft (VEHNT uhl AY
shuhn shaft) a hollow passage
that allows air to move around;
sometimes a fan is built into the
shaft to help move the air

viaduct (VY uh duhkt) a bridge
with a number of very tall
arches joined together for
support

Volkswagen (VOHLKS wag uhn)
a car that is made in Germany

wheel (hweel) a round frame that
turns around a central rod

FURTHER READING

Alth, Max. *Motorcycles and Motorcycling.* New York: F. Watts, Inc., 1979. 90pp.

Broekel, Ray. *Trains.* Chicago: Childrens Press, 1981.

Cave, Ron. *Trains.* New York: Gloucester Press, 1982.

Dixon, Malcolm. *On the Road.* New York: Bookwright Press, 1983.

Gilleo, Alma. *Land Travel From the Beginning.* Elgin, Illinois: Child's World, 1977. 32pp.

Hilton, Suzanne. *Getting There: Frontier Travel Without Power.* Philadelphia: Westminster, 1980.

Jay, Michael. *Cars.* New York: F. Watts, 1982.

Knight, David C. *From Log Roller to Lunar Rover; the Story of Wheels.* New York: Parents Magazine Press, 1974.

Lambert, Laurie and David Lambert. *The Wonderful World of Transportation.* Garden City, New York: Doubleday and Company, Inc., 1969. 96pp.

Lord, Beman. *Look at Cars.* rev. ed. New York: Walck, 1970. 48pp.

Mitgutsch, Ali. *World on Wheels: Rolling Along From Ancient to Modern Times.* New York: Western Publishing Company, Inc., 1975.

Nentle, Jerolyn Ann. *Big Rigs.* Mankato, Minnesota: Crestwood House, 1983.

Quackenbush, Robert. *City Trucks.* Chicago: A. Whitman, 1981.

Richards, Kenneth. *The Story of the Conestoga Wagon.* Chicago: Children's Press, 1970. 32pp.

Rutland, Jonathan. *Exploring the World of Speed*. New York: F. Watts, Inc., 1979.

Sattler, Helen R. *Train Whistles*. New York: Lothrop, Lee and Shepard Company, 1977. 32pp.

Sheffer, H. R. *Tractors.* Mankato, Minnesota: Crestwood House, 1983.

Snow, Richard. *The Iron Road – A Portrait of American Railroading*. New York: Four Winds Press, 1978. 90pp.

Unstead, R. J. *Travel By Road Through the Ages*. Chester Springs, Pennsylvania: Dufour, 1967.

White, Ron. *All Kinds of Trains*. New York: Grosset and Dunlap, 1972.

Young, Frank. *Automobile, from Prototype to Scrapyard.* New York: Gloucester Press, 1982.

Zehavi, A. M., ed. *The Complete Junior Encyclopedia of Transportation*. New York: F. Watts, Inc., 1973.

Zim, Herbert and James R. Skelly. *Trucks*. New York: William Morrow and Company, 1970. 64pp.

QUESTIONS TO THINK ABOUT

The History of Land Travel

Do you remember?

What were some of the ways early people moved heavy loads?

Name some animals that are used to carry things today.

What animal can travel in the desert?

What were the first wheels like?

About how far could a stagecoach go in a day?

Find out about . . .

Animals used for travel. What animals are used to carry people? What animals carry loads on their backs? What animals pull heavy loads? In what parts of the world are these animals used?

Carts and wagons. How are carts and wagons made? What do you need besides wheels? What holds the wheels and lets them turn?

Stagecoaches. When were stagecoaches used in the United States? What cities did they go to? Over what land did they travel? What was a stagecoach trip like?

Two Wheelers

Do you remember?

What were the first bicycles like?

What was the Hobby Horse? When was it used?

Who was Pierre Micheaux? What did he do?

Who made the first motorcycle with a gas engine?

What are most motorcycles with sidecars used for today?

What country is known for making motorcycles?

Find out about . . .

Early bicycles. What were some of the early bicycles like? Who made them? How did they work? Were they easy to ride?

Gottlieb Daimler. When did he live? What were some of the things he built? Why was he important?

Motorcycles. What are some of the different kinds of motorcycles made today? Where are they made? What is a moped? How does it differ from a motorcycle?

Cars

Do you remember?

Name at least six countries that make cars. Can you name the cars?

What did the first cars look like?

What German men made early cars?

How did the Stanley Steamer differ from other early cars?

What was special about the Model T Ford?

What vehicle can be used on sand? On snow?

What is an earth mover? What is it used for?

Find out about . . .

Early car makers. Gottlieb Daimler, Karl Benz, and Henry Ford were three of the early car makers. Who were some of the others? What did each person do or make that was special? Which of them started companies that still make cars today?

Grand Prix racing. Where are Grand Prix races held? What kind of ground do the cars race over? How far do they race? Who are some of the best drivers? What are some other important car races?

Vans and Trucks

Do you remember?

Name as many different kinds of vans and trucks as you can.

What are trailer trucks? How are they different from other trucks?

What is a tank truck? What can it carry?

How was the Space Shuttle moved?

What kind of truck carries cars? How many cars can it move?

Why are earth-moving machines moved by truck?

Find out about . . .

CB radio. Many truck drivers use citizens band radios, or CB radios. What is a CB radio? Why do truck drivers use them? What are some of the special rules for using CB radios? What are some of the special words drivers use on the radio?

Truck driving. How can a person become a truck driver? What is the life of a truck driver like? What are some of the different kinds of jobs truck drivers do? What are some good and bad things about driving to make a living?

Buses

Do you remember?

What is a double decker bus? What city still has double deckers?

About how long ago did people start using buses?

What were the first buses like? What made them move?

Why was it sometimes cold or wet at the top of an old double decker?

How does a motor coach differ from a city bus?

Why might people want to travel by motor coach instead of by train?

Find out about . . .

Early buses. What were the earliest buses like? What cities first had buses? Who invented buses?

Motor coaches. What are some of the big motor coach companies? Where can you go by motor coach? How much do trips cost? What is a modern motor coach like? What are some good things about traveling by motor coach?

Roads

Do you remember?

What did the Romans use to make roads?

What were roads like about 500 years ago?

What did people have to do at a turnpike gate?

How were streets made in some old towns and cities?

What is a superhighway? How is it different from other roads?

Name the three main kinds of bridges.

Why must tunnels have ventilation shafts? How do they work?

Find out about . . .

The Cumberland Road. This was an important road built long ago in the United States. When was it built? Why? Where did it go? How did it help people?

Famous bridges. The Brooklyn Bridge, the Golden Gate Bridge, and the New River Gorge Bridge are three important bridges in the United States. Where are they? What do they cross? What kind of bridge is each? How long are they?

Railways

Do you remember?

What were the first railways built for?

What is a freight train?

What happens at a container depot?

What are three different kinds of locomotives? Which is the oldest kind?

What was Puffing Billy?

What did Tom Thumb race with? Who won?

Where was the first railway for passengers built?

Find out about . . .

Early American trains. Who built the first locomotive in the United States? When? When and where did the first train service start? What were the first trains like? When was the first coast to coast railway built?

Modern trains. What is the world's fastest train? How fast can it go? Where is it? What are some things you can find on modern passenger trains? What is AMTRAK? What does it do?

City Transport

Do you remember?

What is a subway? Why is it a good way to travel in a city?

What was the first city to have a subway?

What are streetcars? How were early streetcars powered?

What city has cable cars?

What is a trolleybus like?

How can you tell if a car is a taxicab?

What is a rickshaw?

Find out about . . .

Subways. What was the first American city to have a subway? What other cities have subways? Is there a subway where you live? Where can you go by subway?

Rickshaws. What countries have rickshaws? What are some different kinds of rickshaws?

City travel. Name as many ways of getting around in a city as you can. What are the good things and bad things about each way? What kind of city transport do you like best? Why?

PROJECTS

Project — A History of Land Travel

Make your own "History of Land Travel" poster. You can use the pictures on pages 6–7 of this book as a model. First, collect pictures and drawings from old magazines or draw some of your own. Try to get as many different kinds of old and new ways of land travel as you can.

Arrange your pictures on a large piece of posterboard. For a really big poster you might want to use two pieces of posterboard together. Make sure you paste on your pictures in the right order. They should be arranged from the oldest to the newest kind of travel. Label each picture with the date or time that kind of travel was used.

Project — A Museum Trip

Many museums have collections of old carriages, cars, trains, and so on. Find out if there is a museum like this near you. Take a trip to the museum and look at its collection. Some museums will let you sit in or even ride in their old vehicles. If you can, get a museum guide to show you around and tell you about the vehicles you see.

INDEX

Photo Credits: All-Sport Photographic Ltd.; Alfa Romeo (Gt. Britain) Ltd; Austin Rover Group Ltd; Bedford Commercial Vehicles; British Tourist Authority; Canadian Pacific; Citroen Cars Ltd; Colorsport; Godfrey Davis Europcar Ltd; Douglas Dickins; Mary Evans; Fiore; Ford Motor Co. Ltd.; Robert Harding; J.M. Jarvis; JCB Sales Ltd; LAT; London Transport; J.G. Mason; National Coal Board; National Motor Museum; Peter Newark's Western Americana; Novosti; Picturepoint Ltd; Paul Popper; SAAB (Gt. Britain) Ltd.; S.N.C.F.; Swiss National Tourist Office; Union Pacific; VAG (UK) Ltd.; ZEFA.

Front cover: Joseph Blumstein.

Illustrations: Jim Bamber; Eddie Brockwell; Robert Burns; Dick Eastland; Dan Escott; Bryan Evans; Elizabeth Graham-Yool; Colin Hawkins; Richard Hook; Eric Jewell; Roger Phillips; Mike Roffe; Barry Salter; Michael Whelply.

Vol. 12